THE
Heart
& THE *Art*
of
Songwriting

David Baroni

THE HEART AND THE ART OF SONGWRITING
By David P. Baroni
Copyright 2011 By Kingdomsongs Inc.
2nd Edition printed 2015
davidbaroni.com

Book cover and page design by Shannon Crowley,
Treasure Image & Publishing - TreasureImagePublishing.com

Table of Contents

Thanks and Dedication:

Thank you!

To all the songwriters who have inspired me-from Lennon and McCartney's "I Wanna Hold Your Hand" to Thomas Dorsey's "Precious Lord Take My Hand." Thank you Stevie Wonder, James Taylor, Twila Paris, Joni Mitchell, Pat Metheny, Andrae Crouch, Becker and Fagan, Kelly Willard, Darrell Evans, Regie Hamm, Michael Kelly Blanchard, Dave Grusin, Herbie Hancock, Bobby McFerrin, Gary Oliver, Steve Fry, Mozart, Handel, the Gershwins, Jimmy Webb, Johnny Mercer, and everyone I have ever co-written with.

Dedicated to my life's partner, the one who has heard the first drafts of most of my songs before anyone else, the mother of our children, the love of my life and the joy of our home, Rita Phillips Baroni.

Eternal gratitude to my Heavenly Father, Jesus the Son and the Holy Spirit.

> *"The Lord is my strength and my shield;*
> *my heart trusts in Him, and I am helped;*
> *therefore my heart exults, and with my*
> *song I shall thank Him." (Psalms 28:7)*

INTRODUCTION

I have written songs since I was 9 or 10 years old, when I wrote my first song about a visit to Planet X. Mercifully I don't remember the song, which was inspired by the shelves filled with the science fiction books that I had discovered at the public library in my small town of Natchez, Mississippi; but I do remember the wonderful sense of achievement and accomplishment of marrying words with music to convey an idea. I was captivated; I was hooked!

Most of the songs that I attempted in my teen years were sappy, angst-ridden and well, adolescent love songs; with the exception of one heavy metal song written to warn against the evils of marijuana with the catchy title "Cannabis Sativa" (the latin word for pot.) I also remember writing a mysterious, minor-chord filled mystical song with lyrics I didn't understand called "Nightbreeze." I think that was my first foray into what I would now call a spiritual or prophetic song; though I didn't realize it at the time.

I was a senior in high school when I realized that I would not be tall enough to play pro basketball, and I chose music as my vocation instead of sports. Since that time I have traveled and sung my songs all over the world, many artists have recorded my songs, and I have known the thrill of hearing them on the radio and seeing them performed on television. How wonderful to get letters and emails from people who have been impacted positively from the songs I have been inspired to write. What a joy to hear congregations lift up their voices and sing my songs! It's especially nice to be an anonymous face in the crowd and the worship team and choir doesn't even know that they are singing a song I wrote! (Of course, I don't mind the compliments and "attaboys" when they find out that I wrote the song!)

Here are some of the things I have learned in my years of songwriting. We will examine some of the key ingredients in the best songs; the tips, tricks and tools. Good songwriting is a craft, it's an art. We'll look into what to do with the songs once they are finished, and I will share about the heart of the matter- the matter of the heart! You will also read some stories behind the songs as I recount the adventures, triumphs and trials that were the inspiration for some of the songs I have written. My faith in Jesus Christ is inextricably woven into my point of view about songwriting, but I trust that the principles I have learned will be valuable to you no matter where you are on your spiritual journey.

I believe that you will find this book interesting, fun, helpful, and most of all... inspiring. Let's begin, shall we?

THE POWER OF SONG

There is a saying in the creative community here in Nashville TN, Music City USA, "It all starts with a song."

That saying, of course, was intended to convey the importance of having a good song to start with in the creative/commercial process of going into the studio, producing the project, marketing it to radio, television, film and the internet, and trying to make sure the artist performing the song gets the maximum exposure and sells records. Ultimately the artists' longevity in the entertainment business depends on, among other things, having memorable, well-crafted songs. Clever production methods and powerful vocals can only go so far to disguise a poorly written song. The song is the thing!

Scottish writer and politician, Andrew Fletcher said: "Let me make the songs of a nation and I care not who makes its laws." How many of us have stood with tears in our eyes and lumps in our throats as we sing our national anthem. Songs have a way of helping ideas and ideals travel from our heads to our hearts.

I believe that the people of God would do well to remember the importance of God's gift of song to us.

God, our Father and our Creator, caused the universe (which means "one word") to come into being by the power of His Word, His Voice. He spoke creation into being. Some theologians suggest that God actually *sung* the universe into existence. Talk about a powerful song... download that!

Words are important, they are much more powerful than most of us realize. The words we speak can cause changes in the people who listen to us. In the Bible the book of Proverbs says, *"Death and life are in the power of the tongue and they that love it (to talk) shall eat the fruit thereof."*

How many times have you replayed in your mind words that were spoken to you or about you- some good, some maybe not so good. Sticks and stones may break your bones but words, indeed, can wound your very soul. Conversely, well-spoken words can uplift and encourage you and change the way you view life, God and yourself. Words have power!

Music is also a very dynamic gift. Music can change the atmosphere, penetrate our defenses and affect emotional, spiritual and even physical changes in the hearer. So what happens when we combine Spirit-inspired words with Spirit-inspired music? We experience *the power of song.*

Most believers in Jesus have no problem believing that they hear from God (indirectly at least) through their pastor's sermon, message or homily. I believe that though the above is an important means of receiving the Word of the Lord, there are many other ways that God speaks to us today.

God speaks to us through His creation *"the heavens are telling the glory of God,"* through our spouses, through our friends, children, circumstances, quiet time with His Word, and also through corporate song.

Psalms 133 talks about the blessing of God's people being in unity. When we sing God breathed songs together corporately there is at least a threefold blessing that is received and given.

1. **The power of the words that we sing.** Many songs are filled with powerful truth and can give us a clearer revelation of Who Jesus is, and Who He is in us! There is a creative power that is released as we lift our voices in faith and declare in song the words inspired by the Holy Spirit.

2. **The power of the music.** David played his instrument before King Saul, and the evil spirits tormenting Saul had to flee. Holy Spirit inspired music brings the atmosphere of heaven to earth and helps us to hear the spiritual sounds of the Kingdom of God come to earth!

3. **The power of unity.** In the West, where the exalting of individualism has too much importance, it is refreshing and vital that we remember that we belong to something much greater than ourselves. Again the 133rd Psalm, *"Behold how good and how pleasant it is for brothers (and sisters) to dwell together in unity. It is like the oil that flows down the beard and the robes of Aaron (we are a royal priesthood through Christ). For **there** (the place of unity) the Lord commands the blessing: even life forevermore!"* (Emphases and parentheses mine)

If one person singing a song can melt a hard heart and help others to focus on the solution instead of the problem, just imagine what power is released when many of us lift our voices together in love and praise to our God through Jesus Christ. Indeed, those praises become a throne for the King of kings as He makes Himself known in our midst. The Lord is our Strength and our **Song**!

WHAT MAKES A SONG GOOD?

The best songs can be as varied musically as Lagos is different from Stockholm, yet most good songs have a few key things in common. Great songs...

1.   Grab you
2.   Move you
3.   Hold you
4.   Stay with you

One complaint I have heard about some contemporary music is that it doesn't sound fresh- that there is a sameness and staleness in the arrangements. The production is formulaic. The lyrics are trite and predictable. The sentiments expressed in the song may be true and probably heartfelt, but the unasked question that many listeners have is "So what?"

Great Songs GRAB You

There is an infectious, joy-filled piano intro to a song that Natalie Cole performs called "This Will Be An Everlasting Love" that catches my ear and starts my toes tapping from the first note... every time I hear it! The production is replete with soaring strings, wailing harmonies, a counterpoint gospel electric piano sound, a tight brass arrangement and a cool sounding conga drum, and it all is built upon the foundation of that soulful and exuberant piano riff.

Take a listen with headphones on sometime to hear how the acoustic and electric pianos complement each other. Of course, it doesn't hurt that Natalie Cole is a great singer and that the song is a well-written happy song about (what else?) love! Many movie soundtracks feature this song right in the beginning of the film to establish a great mood, or that piano intro starts playing toward the end of the film-just when things finally go right for the main character. This song *grabs* you!

Great Songs MOVE You

Music is a gift to help people express and feel emotions. As I write this chapter I am in Nigeria having just spent several days with some of the most celebrative, emotional, exuberant, passionate folks on the planet. Yesterday, we had a celebration time and a time of thanksgiving in a local church that had just sponsored a very successful all-night festival attended by between 40,000 and 50,000 people. It was a huge undertaking involving great sacrifice from literally hundreds of volunteers who undertook the J.A.M. (Jesus And Me) Megafest as a labor of love for God, the city of Abuja and the nation of Nigeria.

I wish you could have been there at the "after-party" service at House on the Rock-The Refuge Church yesterday morning. The music, the songs and the singers MOVED us! Nothing was held back, and the primary emotional evocations were joy and gratitude.

Obviously the emotional content of songs don't just stay at joy and celebration. I have a song lyric that says "If I never knew sorrow, I could never be comforted." Though well-crafted songs can help the listener transcend the cares and struggles of ordinary life, the best songs are not just well-written. The songs that touch the heart the most are born in pain and adversity, yet most of those songs offer a sense of hope as well.

One reason I was so moved by the songs of my Nigerian brothers and sisters is because, though I am limited in my understanding because I am only a visitor here, I have a sense of the struggles that these precious men and women, especially the older ones, have endured. The Bible says "Comfort one another with the comfort that you are comforted with." It's scary and humbling to be needy; to need help, to need comfort. But it is wonderful when God encourages us as only He can! One of my favorite songs is a song co-written by me and my friend Wayne Tate called **"Faithful God."** Notice especially the three lines in bold at the end of the verse.

As the sun is reborn and a beautiful morning
Reminds me of Your faithfulness to me
Through the long lonely night when the
darkness hid the light You gave me grace to
trust and now I see
Even when it's hard to believe
Even when our hope seems all gone
There has never been a night without a dawn

I have had *"long lonely nights when the darkness hid the light."* I've also seen, just when I was about to give up hope, a glimmer of light, a lightening of the horizon as night surrenders to a new day and I have been made partaker of God's mercies which are "new every morning."

The comfort you have received can move others to dare to hope again.

I remember very distinctly driving down the road thinking about the songs of hymn writer Fanny Crosby. She wrote "Blessed Assurance," "Christ the Lord Is Risen Today," and *8,000* other songs! She was blinded by an incompetent doctor at 6 weeks of age, yet she said, "It seemed intended by the blessed providence of God that I should be blind all my life, and I thank Him for the dispensation. If perfect earthly sight were offered me tomorrow I would not accept it. I might not have sung hymns to the praise of God if I had been distracted by the beautiful and interesting things about me."

I also thought about Horatio Spafford who wrote the beloved hymn of comfort "It Is Well With My Soul." I cried to the Lord, "God, I want to write songs like those hymn writers wrote, songs that touch people deeply." He replied, "Are you aware of the suffering those writers went through?" I gulped and said, "Hold that prayer for a moment Lord and let me think about this!"

Not all songs are written to effect the listener in dramatic ways (nor should they be.) There are myriad emotions and many ways to be moved by a song- the main thing is that a good song should help us feel, great songs *move* us.

Great Songs HOLD You

Those of you who watch "American Idol" (or "Australian Idol" or "Indonesian Idol" or _____ (insert your country here) probably have experienced what my wife Rita and I have as we occasionally watched the show. Invariably one or more of the performers fail to keep our interest partway through the song. It falls flat and almost everybody knows it. Then one of the judges says, "Now look, last week you brought it, you laid it down, but this week… I don't know man; I don't think the song was right for you- you just didn't take us anywhere, you didn't hold our attention."

What could be true in regards to a performance of a song can also be true in the writing of a song. I must confess that at times I would start out well with a song I was writing. The first verse and maybe even the chorus flowed; the melody was "hook-y" and the music and rhythm was working well; then… well, then nothing! So I would force another verse-some lyrics or music that deep down I knew that I was just settling for. The song "had me at hello" but because of my fatigue or laziness it didn't *keep* me (or potential listeners), because I gave up and took the easy way out and ended up with a mediocre, or even a bad song, or worse, a "so-what?" song.

If you get tired while writing or co-writing you can always record what you have and take a break, even overnight or several days, and come back to it with fresh ears and ideas later.

If you have a great start to what you think could be a great song, don't settle for less than just the right words, the perfect melody or chord changes just because it gets difficult. Just take a break! Then come back and finish that keeper song that keeps people listening from start to finish. I have even waited *years* to finish a few songs. Sometimes your life experience has to catch up with what you are writing. Honor the song and make it the best it can be-a keeper song that holds the listener the whole way through.

Great Songs STAY WITH You

Great songs are like a great speech. In a good speech there usually is an introduction, the main body of the speech and the conclusion.

In the introduction the person giving the speech tells the audience what he or she is about to say. In the body of the speech, she says it. In the conclusion, the speaker tells them what she just told them. It looks like this:

> ***Introduction***: Tell them what you are about to tell them
>
> ***Body***: Tell them
>
> ***Conclusion***: Sum it up; tell them what you just told them.

Many of my songs have followed this pattern; though most of the time it was an instinctive rather than conscious intention on my part.

In the verse, I set up the chorus. I *introduce* the theme that I want the song to be about. Then toward the end of the verse I usually have a line or two that was somewhat different in melody and chord structure that would lead nicely into the chorus. These lines are commonly called the pre-chorus today. So the verse (introduction) builds to the pre-chorus (which I consider still part of the verse) which climaxes into the chorus (the main theme, the body) of the song.

"Take Me to the Bridge"

Sometimes the fresh musical departure of a cool bridge can help keep the listener interested and give them a takeaway, something in the song that stays with them.

Are you with me so far? Let's do a quick review.

The verse is the introduction. Musically and lyrically I tell the listener (the audience) what I am about to tell them. In the chorus I *tell* them (the *body*, the main purpose of the song or speech). A chorus should convey the main idea of the song. The more memorable it is...the catchier the melody and words and chords and rhythm are-the better.

So what about the bridge? Before we go to the bridge I want to add that many songs today don't have (or need) bridges. This is a personal preference of mine to include bridges in most of my songs. Why? Well, they are a challenge musically to me. I love to come up with something different sometimes to keep myself engaged musically and lyrically in the creative process.

To write a cool bridge is fun! The bridge also is a great way to sum up what you feel the song is conveying. The bridge, like the *conclusion* of a good speech, tells the listener what they just heard in the verse and the chorus. It reinforces, sometimes with powerful effect, what the verse and chorus were about. Good songs that stay with you paint pictures, tell stories and keep you humming the melody even when you are not conscious of it.

Of course, bad songs can get stuck in your brain too. Why is that? I believe it's because there is a gift of memory that God placed inherently in the gift of music. He put it there, in my humble and accurate opinion, to help His children remember Who He is, His promises, His word. That's why I want to be a good steward of the songwriting gift, and hopefully write songs that are worth remembering, that stay with the listener!

More About The Verse, Chorus, Bridge

As I mentioned earlier, a good song doesn't have to have a bridge, it doesn't even have to have a verse! Here is an example of a song I wrote (my most popular one on the CCLI charts as a matter of fact) that is just a chorus. This song was inspired, I believe, by the Holy Spirit at the end of a worship service. I sang it spontaneously right after a pastor's message. It was written on the spot and has been recorded not only by me, but by Paul Wilbur, Michael W. Smith, Selah, Natalie Grant and several others. It has been recorded in Spanish and Italian.

O draw me Lord
O draw me Lord
O draw me Lord
And I'll run after You

This song has a grand total of nine words, ten if you count the contraction as two words. When I sing it the second time through I change the melody of the last line. I also change pronouns in a worship service sometimes. We sing "O draw *us* Lord… and *we'll* run after You."

When I change the pronoun once more from "*us*" to "*them*" ("O draw *them* Lord and *they'll* run after You") *it* turns the song from a personal prayer (O draw *me)* and a prayer for unity (O draw *us)* into an intercessory prayer for people who don't know the Love of God through Jesus yet.

O draw *them* Lord and they'll run after You

My first "live" recording of the song, those nine words, was almost *ten minutes long*!

Now I am not nearly clever enough to have thought of all that in those spontaneous moments when the Holy Spirit inspired the original chorus. It has been through years of singing the song and listening for the Spirit's direction that the song has evolved into that three-part prayer, but the basic form of the song is still that it is "just" a chorus. It stands alone just fine.

I Rest In You (Not Afraid)

Here is another example of a song that has just three parts: a verse, a chorus and a bridge. It is a special song inspired in Lagos, Nigeria called "I Rest In You (Not Afraid.)."

I had been in Africa for almost two weeks. I had sung and taught in Abuja and Kaduna in northern Nigeria, and (for the last week of the trip) in the sprawling Lagos area. The ministry had gone exceptionally well, but two weeks is a long time to be away from my wife and family, and by the last day of ministry I was ready to be back home in good-ole Franklin, Tennessee.

So, wearily I rode in the car driven by my friend (and sometimes co-writer) Kunle Fadahunsi across town to the Rose of Sharon Church pastored by Olatunde Odusote. We call him Rev. Doc.

It was only 7:30 in the morning, painfully early for this musician. I was tired and homesick and frankly wanted to get the day over with and get home to Rita. But God gives grace…

As Kunle and I walked into the church, Reverend Doc, a wonderful, strong and gentle man of God, was leading some of the church volunteers in worship before the service started. I was going to minister in two morning services. The people were singing with such passion, and there was such an overwhelming, obvious, tangible sense of the Presence of the Lord in that place that I was instantaneously refreshed; not just emotionally but *physically!*

What had happened? Well, the Psalms say that God is enthroned in, inhabits, lives in, makes Himself known in the praises of His people (Psalms 22:3) The word also says that there are times of refreshing that come from the *Presence of the Lord* and in His

Presence is fullness of joy, at His right Hand are pleasures forevermore!

Led by Rev. Doc, the believers in Jesus were singing praises that He made Himself at home in. As we experienced His Manifest Presence, we were refreshed and experienced fullness of joy!

All this, and the church service hadn't even started yet. The first service went well. We took a short break and a different group of folks from the congregation gathered for the second service. At the end of the meeting Pastor Odusote (Doc) got up to encourage the people and, I thought, dismiss the service.

But God wasn't through...

Reverend Doc started singing spontaneously a new song inspired by the Holy Spirit. God is the best songwriter by far who ever was or will be, and He is the reason for any impact songs have had on people!

Doc sang a simple melody and this simple phrase:

*"I rest in You Oh Lord, I trust in You Oh God,
I'm not afraid anymore; I'm not afraid
anymore."*

He sang it acapella. He sang it again. People joined in. "I rest in You Oh Lord…" The music team joined in, playing a simple "Heart and Soul" chord progression. (In the key of "F" the chords would be **F, Dm7, Gm7, Bb/C**) We "owned" the song; the words were not only coming from Rev. Doc, we all sang them and meant them and those words became a powerful declaration of faith: "I'm not afraid anymore."

As I wrote in the first chapter of this book "The Power of Song" this spontaneously inspired song was a prophetic proclamation in the middle of Lagos. The people were set free from fear by the grace of God and the Power of the Name of Jesus through the words of faith we were singing!

The next day, the day before I returned to America, Kunle and I were remembering the wonderful time we had on Sunday, and we started talking about Doc's song. Before we knew it, we were inspired to write a verse. We called Doc to ask if we could put our verse with his chorus and he graciously and excitedly said yes. Great things happen in the Kingdom of God when we don't worry about who gets the credit and we give God the honor and the glory! (I know some songwriters who actually count the words that they contribute to a song in order to split songwriter percentages, and I suppose in some cases that could be valid for some personality types, but as we say in Mississippi "Oh for cryin' out loud!")

So, in this case, the chorus was written first. If you notice the verse lyrics below, it follows the speech-giving formula of using the verse as an introduction, a "reason why" that builds into the chorus.

Then a bit later, Kunle and I added the bridge which reinforces scripturally and emotionally the reason why we can rest and not be afraid. As we sing the bridge we are literally and spiritually singing the Word of God to our own souls!

Here is the song, notice the three parts:

"I Rest In You (Not Afraid)"

Olatunde Odusote/ David Baroni/ Kunle Fadahunsi

Verse:
When I'm down, darkness all around
And it seems like no help can be found
Fear wants in, I feel like giving in
Oh what can I do?
Then I cry to God Most High
Who gives me grace to say

Chorus:
I rest in You oh Lord
I trust in You oh God
I'm not afraid anymore
I'm not afraid anymore
(repeat)

Bridge:
Return to your rest oh my soul
Return to your rest oh my soul
For the Lord will be faithful to you
For the Lord will be faithful to you

Remember that a good song doesn't have to have a Bridge; it doesn't even have to have a verse! I want to add one more observation about the bridge to "I Rest In You" before we move on to look at some practical elements of a good song. Originally I just sang each line of the song one time so the bridge looked like this:

Return to your rest Oh my soul
For the Lord will be faithful to you

Now there is nothing wrong with writing or singing it that way but in a rehearsal one day I accidentally sang each line twice. There was something about repeating each line that made the bridge sentiment more powerful. We added a bass line that walked up with each phrase and it builds into the chorus nicely:

Bb   **C**

Return to your rest oh my soul

Bb/D   **C/E**

Return to your rest oh my soul

37

Sometimes a repeated line in a song can have the same effect as it did on the slaves who sang in the fields in those days when slavery was still accepted in the U.S. Singing it over and over can help make the message become part of you. We tap into the power of the words that we speak.

Proverbs says that death and life are in the power of the tongue and they that love it (to talk) shall eat the fruit thereof. As I said in the first chapter, words are powerful and if you begin to really own, really believe what you are singing, (provided, of course, that it really is true) it is a wonderful way to impart God's truth and promises, His Word, to yourself and those who hear you! It also gets your mind off of the tedious "field work" that is sometimes a part of life.

Obviously, as with any good thing, you can over-do repetition as well. The more you write the greater your sense of discernment will be about when to stop repeating phrases. That is also true in worship leading. Sometimes I think I hear the Holy Spirit say, "That's enough already!" Like most things, balance in our lyrical and musical approach is a good idea.

Before we move on to some practical and fundamental elements in a song, I want to tell you another story behind the song.

THE SOUND OF HEAVEN

While in Romania recently, I heard two profound things. Early in the morning after I arrived in Timisoara, I opened the guest room window and heard... nothing! The sound of silence was stunning. No highway noises, people talking, horns beeping...nada! As I tuned my ears to the silence, small sounds were magnified. A bird flew past the window, and I could actually hear it's wings flapping. This experience underscored just how noisy my life usually is. The silence was magical, invigorating. The second sound I heard was also early in the morning. It was also profound. It was a Sound of the Spirit- the Sound of Heaven.

In Genesis, Adam and Eve heard the "*sound* of the Lord God walking in the garden." Some translations say they heard the "*Voice* of the Lord walking..." I love that imagery. The Sound of Heaven is the sound of the vibrant praises of the passionate Romanian believers from the school of worship. It is the sound of the beautiful Ecuadorian dancers I watched as they worshiped the Lord in Quito recently. It is the sound of the Spirit, the sound of worship.

In the book of Acts the disciples heard the "sound as of a rushing mighty wind." I believe that since the day of Pentecost, when the Holy Spirit came to dwell within and empower the church, the sound of heaven has been evident and manifested; made known, in the praises of the people of God! We are more than doing Christian Karaoke when we gather and lift our hearts and voices to the Lord. Jesus is enthroned in our praises and a desperate world can begin to hear, by God's grace, the sound of Eden again. The sound of heaven! These words, along with the music, came pouring to me that August morning in Romania. I shared this song with the people who had gathered from all over Romania the night after I wrote the song.

Sound of Heaven

David Baroni/ Kingdomsongs Inc./ BMI/CCLI

Listen…do you hear it?
There's a sound arising in the earth
Growing stronger… in the nations
It's the sound of worship it's the sound of grace
As a desperate generation seeks His Face

It's the Sound of heaven filling the earth
It's the sound of freedom it's the sound of Love
The Breath of God is blowing bringing life to
these dry bones
Blow Wind blow
Flow River flow
Fill the earth… with the sound of heaven

Listen… can you feel it?
There's a sound arising in this place
Getting louder… by the minute
It's the sound of passion it's the sound of joy
It's the very Life of Jesus in our praise!

It's the Sound of heaven filling the earth
It's the sound of freedom it's the sound of Love
The breath of God is blowing bringing life to
these dry bones
Blow Wind blow

Flow river flow
Fill the earth… with the sound of heaven

It's the sound of unity
And true humility
The sound of power
And healing in His name
You can hear it in the silence and the mighty
rushing wind
The voice of God is walking in the garden again!

Words and Music: The Basics

I love words. Just ask my wife. Words are part of my primary love language. I also value words. Words have meaning. Words are important.

There are two main components of most songs with vocals: lyrics and music. Let's look first at how to put words together in creative and accessible ways. Here are six attributes of a well-crafted lyric:

1. **Scriptural (True)**

2. **Relevant (Fresh)**

3. **Concise**

4. **Accessible**

5. **Consistent (Staying with one theme)**

6. **Flowing With the Music**

Scriptural (True)

Most of the songs I have written have been in the "praise and worship" genre; in other words, these have been songs that are written not just for people to hear but for people to *sing* in corporate gatherings such as church worship meetings and camps and conferences. I want to write songs that are true to scripture, the Bible, for a number of reasons, the main one being that I believe what Jesus said, "And you shall know the truth and the truth shall make you free."

This principle of truth holds true no matter what genre of song; whether praise and worship, pop, country, R and B, Hip-Hop, etc.; even instrumental songs! (Truth can be displayed without words; just look at a beautiful sunrise or listen to an anointed instrumental song.) For the purposes of this book, however, I am focusing primarily on praise and worship songs. As a lover of God and a believer in the power of words, the clearer the truth is communicated in a song, the stronger that song is.

However, I am not saying that the songwriter needs to quote verbatim from the Bible in his or her song. Sometimes doing that is a good thing; for example, I use paraphrases of the psalms all the time in my writing. My point is that the lyric should have its basis in truth.

For those of you who are thinking "well...duh," you would be amazed at some of the errant theology that is rampant in praise and worship songs. Indeed, I have written songs years ago that cause me to cringe when I think about them today, because my theological perspective has matured as I have grown in my walk with the Lord. It's a good thing that God is patient with us.

One example I will give of using scripture, yet not quoting it verbatim is in the previously mentioned song, "I Rest In You."

> *Return to your rest O my soul*
> *Return to your rest O my soul*
> *For the Lord will be faithful to you*
> *For the Lord will be faithful to you*

The bridge of that song is taken from Psalms 116:7, *"Return to your rest O my soul, for the Lord has dealt bountifully with you."* Notice that in the first line (which is repeated) the lyric is taken directly from that passage of scripture. It is verbatim. However, instead of using the second half of the scripture, the next line is rendered *"For the Lord will be faithful to you."*

We as the songwriters felt that the second line didn't have to be the literal "...for the Lord has dealt bountifully with you" for a number of reasons. For one thing the word "bountifully" is not a commonly used word these days. It's a good word but in the context of singing a worship song it's old-fashioned, antiquated. Another reason for not quoting the whole passage verbatim is that the tense of the scripture is past tense. We wanted the song to not only be a reminder of God's faithfulness to us in the past, but also that He will continue to be faithful. In fact, "Faithful and True" is one of the very names of God!

Are we taking liberty with the scriptures? No, not if the lyric remains consistent with other revelations of the character of God. Over and over again in the Word of God we are assured that God has been faithful and will be faithful to His children.

One more point about scriptural and true lyrics. There are some that are so afraid that scripture will be violated that they become self-appointed custodians of the Bible (of course, only the version of the Bible that they and their circle approves of). It is good to have a zeal for truth in this relativistic society, but a fearful exclusive attitude is contrary to the character of Christ. Paul wrote in 2 Corinthians 3:6 *"...for the letter kills, but the Spirit gives life."* God's goal in sending His Son Jesus, the Word made flesh, was to reconcile fallen mankind to Himself. God broke 400 years of silence between the end of the Old Testament and the beginning of the new in a very dramatic fashion. *He sent His very voice!* Why? Because God is passionate about communication, and that is because communication is an outflow of relationship. God is intent on living in relationship with His people! The truth sets free and the Spirit gives life!

Relevant (Fresh, Creative)

One of my favorite songs has not been recorded yet, and hasn't been heard by many people. It is a song called "I'm Okay Today." It is not designed to be sung by a congregation. In fact, one reason I like it so much is that it is truth that the hearer will have to think about. It's subtle, but powerful.

"Okay Today"

Joy and pain
Sun in the rain
Crazy sane
At the same time
I have swung
On the pendulum
From the silence to the scream
But life is less in the extremes
Than in between

(Chorus)
I'm okay today
Let tomorrow take tomorrow
I can live today
I will dream I will dance

I'll let go-take a chance
And love will carry me
Love will carry me
Today

Yesterday
Has gone away
And all that's left
Are the memories
But I have now
And grace somehow
To live in color live out loud
I am humble I am proud!

<u>(Chorus)</u>
I'm okay today
Let tomorrow take tomorrow
I can live today
I will dream I will dance
I'll let go-take a chance
I will dream I will dance
I'll let go-take a chance
I will dream I will dance
I'll let go-take a chance
And love will carry me
Love will carry me
Today

"Okay Today"/ David Baroni/ Kingdomsongs Inc.

There are so many things I love about this song. Let's examine it more closely.

(Please forgive me if it seems self-indulgent for me to be in love with one of my own songs. I enjoy the gifts of God, and if I didn't get excited about the creative process of songwriting, then I probably need to find something else to do with my time!)

In the first verse there is not only a cool rhyme scheme;

Joy and pain
Sun in the rain
Crazy sane
At the same time

There is also what I call the "power of paradox." A paradox is two ideas that are found together, yet seem to be opposites. A wise preacher friend of mine said this: "Where you find a paradox my friend, you find God." Jesus said when we *lose* our lives we *find* them. When we *give*, we *receive.* The paradox has power because it confounds our human tendency to have things figured out and it gives the grace of God room to be perceived. When we are *weak*, then we are *strong*.

Let's move to the next lines:

> ***I have swung***
> ***On the pendulum***
> ***From the silence to the scream***
> ***But life is less in the extremes***
> ***Than in-between***

I like these lines because they say something about that which is familiar to most of us; the emotional rollercoaster. Being excited about life one moment, then because of a change in circumstance or a change in our blood-sugar level, being down in the dumps the next moment. It's not necessarily mental illness, it's just life!

Notice that there is a softer rhyme at work. Instead of an exact (some songwriters call them "masculine") rhyme with the word "swung") there is a "feminine" rhyme: the word "pendulum." (By the way, I think this is the only song I have ever written with that word in it!)

Creative and fresh lyrics paint pictures. "I have swung on the pendulum from the silence to the scream." Can't you just see the emotional rollercoaster? Can you *feel* it as well? So far the verse has set up a scenario that is just begging for some explanation. The good songwriter employs that creative tension, lets it build, then just at the right time begins to give some answers. Not all the answers at once, mind you. Life is not like that. One of the faults I have found in my earlier songs is that they are too quick to point to the answer; there is not enough creative tension in them.

So, after swinging from the silence to the scream where do we go? To one of my favorite lines in the song:

But life is less in the extremes than in-between

I like lyrics that cause the listener to do a mental double-take. Look at the line again. "Life is less in the extremes." The implication, the unspoken thought here is that life, satisfaction, peace can be found more easily in the day-to-day and in the ordinary, than in the highs and lows that so many people seem to live for. At least that's what I meant when I wrote it.

Now we go to the chorus: "I'm okay today, let tomorrow take tomorrow." These words remind me of the words of Jesus, "So do not worry about tomorrow; for tomorrow will care for itself." (Matthew 6:34a) Again, the message that is implied is that the singer will be present in the present. How many of us have not been engaged or emotionally available in the present? We are either regretting the past or fearing (or anticipating) the future. In 12-step recovery programs there is a saying: "Take one day at a time." There is a lot of wisdom in that.

The rest of the chorus:

> *I will dream I will dance*
> *I'll let go-take a chance*
> *And love will carry me*
> *Love will carry me*
> *Today*

Toward the end of the chorus there is a positive affirmation to celebrate the good things in life. It is hopeful: "I will dream I will dance." It reminds me of the saying, "Dance like nobody's watching, love like you've never been hurt." It is also an exhortation to trust: "I'll let go," and to take risks: "Take a chance." I love the rhyme scheme and the repetitive melody. To those who haven't heard the song the lines "I will dream, I will dance, I'll let go, take a chance" are sung with a repeating 3 note melody- one note per word. Underneath the melody there is moving a building set of chord changes (check out the audiobook version of this book!) Anyway, trust me; it's pretty cool!

The chorus finally ends with a reason for my faith and hope:

> **And love will carry me**
> **Love will carry me**
> **Today**

Okay, smile! We have made it all the way to verse two. This verse gives more illumination to what was implied in the first verse. In other words it fleshes out the meaning of the song a bit more:

> **Yesterday**
> **Has gone away**

And all that's left
Are the memories
But I have now
And grace somehow
To live in color live out loud
I am humble I am proud!

Again we see an implied confession that the singer has had a tendency to live in the past. It's not all bad, however. There are memories that remain, and they are gifts. Then there is the short but powerful declaration:

"But I have NOW"

Again, I will be present in the present. I will be fully engaged with God, with myself, with the people in my life, with the world.

"...and grace somehow"

I will be present in the present *in His Presence*!

"To live in color live out loud"

This is my favorite line. Before I really started to know how gracious and generous and *for me* that

God is, I just tried to keep the rules, do the right thing and hopefully not be rejected.

I have experienced the trauma of abuse in my youth that, coupled with legalism and a "performance-based-acceptance mindset," tainted my ability to have a healthy awareness of Who God really is and who I am through Jesus Christ. Thank God for godly Christian counseling and most of all, that He loved me enough to be patient with me and show me His love, acceptance and joy.

In living in color and living out loud I am, of course, not advocating selfishness or rebellion. I simply and profoundly want to honor the goodness of my Creator, my Father, by living with an expectation of His goodness. Will we ask for bread and He give us a stone? Of course not.

Then comes the final lines of the verse:

I am humble I am proud!

There's the use of paradox again. Some may argue that one cannot be humble and proud at the same time. The Word says to "rejoice with trembling," that is; celebrate the goodness of God with a sober awareness that we can do nothing to deserve that goodness. I'm O.K today. We all can be. Because of Jesus.

So let's dream and let's dance
Let go and take a chance
Because Love will carry us
Love will carry you...
Today

Before we conclude discussing relevant lyrics let me add one more thing. *Keep it fresh!* Say that He's worthy in a new way without saying the word "worthy." Don't take the easy way out and settle for over-used expressions, no matter how true they may be. I love the song "How He Loves" by John Mark McMillan. From the first lines:

He is jealous for me
Loves like a hurricane I am a tree
Bending beneath the weight of His wind and
mercy

When all of a sudden
I am unaware of this affliction eclipsed by
Glory...

Love it! It's a fresh way to say how powerful the love of God is. There is the use of comparison: God's love- to a hurricane, me- to a bowed-over tree. It paints pictures, not trite at all but sober and powerful. I especially love the line "When all of a sudden I am *unaware* of this affliction eclipsed by glory." Usually in life we are suddenly made *aware* of something. In this line the songwriter changes it around. "I am *unaware* of this affliction eclipsed by glory." The line subliminally reminds me of the hymn "Turn Your Eyes Upon Jesus" especially this part, "...and the things of earth will grow strangely dim in the light of His glory and grace." Let your lyrics out of the box. Dare to color outside the lines. Not merely for the sake of drama or poetry, of course it has to ring true... resist the easy way out; be creative!

More About Words and Music

Concise

Fill this place
With the praise
Of the God
Of all grace
Lift Him High
Glorify
The Ancient of Days
Oh ye saints
Lift Your voice
Lift Your heads
And rejoice
God is here
Fill this place with praise

David Baroni/ Bo Cooper/Integrity Music/ Sunday Shoes Music

I have sung the song "Fill This Place" for years now as an opening song in a worship set or concert. There are several reasons that this song is a good one to begin an evening or morning of congregational worship. It states the wonderfully obvious: "God is here!" Musically the song is palatable and accessible to a lot of age ranges and musical preferences. I believe that the Lord inhabits, makes His Presence known, in the praises of His people (Psalms 22:3.) One of the main reasons I use this song a lot, however, is because it is easy to learn. That is because it is not wordy, the lyrics are *concise.*

Every Word is Important

Don't settle. Find *just* the right word to convey what is in your heart and mind. In the original typesetting for the leadsheet of the song "Fill This Place," the transcriber got one word wrong. He or she put these lines in musical notation:

> *Oh ye saints lift your voice*
> *Lift your **hands** and rejoice*

I must admit, when I first saw that I was steamed. Not that there is anything wrong with saying "lift your *hands*" but that word, that thought, has been so overused. Using the word *heads,*

*Lift your **heads** and rejoice*

has an entirely different, and more powerful connotation. Word choices are important!

The Value of Word Elimination: The Dreaded Eraser!

Early in my songwriting days I learned a great lesson from a friend that I was co-writing with.

Tom Hemby is a wonderfully gifted musician and producer, and he and I got together to write a song. I had some ideas and the room we were writing in had a chalkboard or whiteboard so I started writing something like this: (I will exaggerate it for the sake of the example but the original was almost as bad!)

Once I was a desperate frightened fugitive
I was running away from the light
I was wounded and hurting because of my sin
And stumbling through the cold dark night
It was such a tragedy
I could see no hope for me

Pretty awful, huh? But there was a seed of an idea there and Tom saw it. Co-writing is good for the ego- good for the destruction of pride I should say! Tom got the dreaded eraser and approached my "sacred" writings. Don't be afraid to erase and rewrite! Here is what it looked like:

Desperate   fugitive
running   from the light
wounded   sin
stumbling through the   night
tragedy
no hope for me

Now, let's add one word to the 3rd line; the word "by" and… voila! …a concise verse is born:

Desperate fugitive
Running from the light
Wounded by sin
Stumbling through the night

Tragedy
No hope for me

My favorite line contains only one word: *"Tragedy."* That one word says what originally I intended to say with five words.

Now for you folks that are wondering what in the world happened to the protagonist in the above song, let me comfort you with the words to the chorus:

Now I'll never run away again
Never try to fly against the wind
No I'll never run away again
No more looking for love
'Cause I found it in Him

To rhyme or not to rhyme...

I think the question of whether or not to always use rhyming words is a matter of personal preference. It also depends on the song and what the song "wants." Personally, I love rhyming-the more rhymes the better. There are different forms for words to rhyme: every line rhyming; every other line rhyming, etc. I don't think there is a set formula for it. I will say that internal rhymes are particularly appealing to me. For example let's examine the chorus of my song *"God of All Glory"*

> *God of all glory*
> *God of all grace*
> *Oh the **sight of the light** of the love in*
> *Your Face*
> *Now I rest in Your righteousness*
> *Trust the embrace*
> *Of the God of all glory*
> *God of all grace*

Notice the third line: *"Oh the sight of the light of the love in Your Face."* The words "sight" and "light" sing nicely. I also love alliteration and used it in the continuation of the line *"light of the love..."* In fact the title and main lines of the song have a nice hard "g" alliteration:

> *"God of all glory, God of all grace"*

Before we move on to discussing the next facet of lyric-writing, let me tell a humorous story about one of my songs that got "lost in translation."

As I travel around the world, I am amazed at (and sometimes appalled by) some aspects of the prevalence of American culture. Sometimes, however, we Americans forget that, just like other cultures, we have some peculiarities of speech, slang or colloquialisms that are not easily translated. One time a drummer was teaching a class about a certain error in drumming technique that, if used, would cause you not to "get to third base." The baseball reference got lost in translation. "Do we need to have three bass guitars?"

Usually, the people who have translated my songs do a wonderful job of keeping true to the original meaning, yet making the translation singable and understandable (and musical). It's a challenging thing to translate well- it's not just a matter of inserting the Italian or Russian word where the English word is.

One time at a worship conference in a far away land, a translator had the challenging job of translating the "slangy" song written by me and Kevin Singleton: "Ain't Gonna Let No Rock Outpraise Me" (from the story of Jesus riding into Jerusalem and the religious leaders telling Him to get His disciples to be quiet. Of course Jesus told them that, "If these hold their peace, the very rocks themselves will cry out in their places." The idea being that I don't want a rock to give God the praise that should be coming from me. It's easy to understand from the English version, right? What these dear translators wrote at first (they later changed it to be true to the original intent of the song so it got caught in time) was this:

"I'm not going to let any rock music come between me and my worship to God!" Which is a fine declaration against idolizing a style of music, but it's not exactly what Kevin and I had in mind in the writing of the song!

Accessible

There is a saying that if you are leading and no one is following then you are just taking a walk. Put in a songwriting context: If you are spouting prose and poetry and hiding mysteries within your deep artistic creations that, if you would be honest about it, not even *you* understand; then you are not hitting the mark if your goal is to *communicate*. I am not advocating dumbing down your songs or sapping the fresh creativity from the lyrics; I am simply saying that if people can't understand what you are saying in a song then why say it?

The glorious exceptions to this are songs that are designed to ask but not answer questions. There are songs like that and they have their place. For the sake of this writing, however, we are mainly talking about songs that congregations and audiences will sing, let's focus on having lyrics that are accessible.

Let's take another line-by-line look at the song "Faithful God." Here's the verse. It only has one because it only *needs* one!

As the sun is reborn and a beautiful morning
Reminds me of Your faithfulness to me

Consistent throughout this song is the theme of the sunrise after a long, hard night. "*As the sun is reborn*" is another way to say, "It's morning again." Notice the internal rhyme re*born* and *morn*ing. A paraphrase of the first few lines:

The sun has come up again, it's a beautiful day, and as I see it I remember that God, you have been faithful to me.

Through the long lonely night
When the darkness hid the light

Most good songs have creative tension. It's not all sweetness and light. Neither is life. To pretend otherwise is called denial. The key in songwriting is how much to employ. Too much darkness and the song can easily become morbid. Not enough reality and the song is fluff, like cotton candy. It may be sweet but there is not a lot of nourishment in it.

Most people who have lived any time at all can relate to having long lonely nights when it seemed like light (love, God, help) was nowhere to be found. The next lines give the access point, the place in the song that people can identify with and enter in to what the songwriters are wanting to convey:

> *Even when it's hard to believe*
> *Even when our hope seems all gone*
> *There has never been a night without a dawn*

I can almost hear an old saint say, *"Well...! Preach it brother!"* after those lines! The whole song is summed up in the last line of the verse: *"There has never been a night without a dawn."* That is a fresh way of saying that there will be tough times in life, but as the scripture says, "God is faithful Who will not allow you to be tempted above what you are able to bear, but will with the temptation make a way of escape."

Another way to look at words that are accessible is to substitute the word *honest* for the word accessible, or better yet, *real*. I love the vulnerability that is inherent in a lot of songs today. Writers and artists are saying things in creative and heart-touching ways that connect with people.

When my wife and I sang at the Brooklyn Tabernacle in New York City years ago Pastor Jim Cymbala told us, "The people in this congregation can spot a con a mile away because most of them were cons before they met Jesus!"

People are looking for the real thing and they can see right through the performer's pretense. To be accessible, be understandable and vulnerable. Don't be undiscerning or over-emotional. Be honest and communicate.

Keep it real!

Consistent: Keep To One Theme

What is your song saying? What is it about? Do you have one theme that you stay with throughout the song? Are you like I was when I first started writing; trying to put thoughts from Genesis to Revelation in every song?!

Most songs these days are four to five minutes long. The pop songwriters of yesteryear could say things in less time than that. Because of the constraints of most radio formats, the goal for a hit single was to keep it under 3 minutes.

Sometimes when I do concerts, as was the case this past weekend in Abuja, Nigeria; there are time constraints given to each artist/worship leader. Generally I like that, (unless it is a very short amount of time) because it forces me to edit my songlist and really weigh what I say between songs. I am more able to focus on a theme, to be consistent.

Of course the balance here is that I think we also need times of no time constraints, sometimes (within reason) corporately we need to be able to flow with the Holy Spirit and take our time in His Presence. It depends on the situation. In our personal time with God we don't have to stick to the clock; let it flow!

An example of a song that keeps to one theme in almost every line is my new song "Liquid Love." This song is one of my new favorites partly because, if you will notice, almost every line has something to do with water or liquid. I didn't set out to do it that way. I was in the congregation at a worship time in our church when I received the impression that the healing Presence of Jesus permeated the room and my being and it felt like... well, like liquid Love. (Songwriters should always have the antennae up to catch new song ideas!)

The verse started coming to me right there in the service and I finished the song within a day or two. Some people ask me which comes first to me, the music or the lyrics. Most of the time I hear them together. Sometimes a lyrical idea presents itself and then there are those rare times when the music comes first and the words later. Here are the words to "Liquid Love."

Notice how the whole song focuses on the theme of water; notice also (and I am proud of this) that I don't actually use the word *"water"* until almost the end of the song; in the bridge.

Liquid Love

David Baroni/Kingdomsongs Inc.

Verse 1

Your love is an ocean Your grace like the sea
Your faithfulness wave after wave to me
Your mercy's a fountain
Your peace like a stream
Your joy is a river flowing within me
Flowing within me

Chorus

You wash over me like liquid love
Through the tears and the rain
With your cleansing blood
You pour out Your grace in a healing flood
And wash over me
Wash over me
You wash over me
Like liquid love

Verse 2:

Sometimes I get thirsty my spirit's so dry
Surrounded by desert no clouds in the sky
The wind gently whispers
And I call Your Name
I'm suddenly laughing out loud in the rain
I dance in the rain (repeat chorus)

Bridge

To the tired and thirsty soul
In a dry and weary land
There's One Who will heal you
Save you and fill you
Come to the water and drink
Come to the water and drink
Then you will sing

Chorus

You wash over me like liquid love
Through the tears and the rain
With your cleansing blood
You pour out Your grace in a healing flood
And wash over me
Wash over me
You wash over me
Like liquid love

Look at all the words that are either synonyms for something liquid or describe the effects of something liquid or the effects of the absence of liquid:

ocean, sea, wave after wave, fountain, stream,
river, flowing, liquid, tears, rain, cleansing
blood, pour, healing flood, wash,
thirsty, dry, desert, clouds, rain, water, drink

Notice also that there are very few repeated words, yet the song stays true to its theme. I will add that this song is exceptionally thematic, most songs don't have lyrics with that strong of an emphasis on the title, however, this gives you a good idea of what I mean by being consistent.

In short, resist the temptation to overdo it by trying to cover too many ideas in one song. Decide what the song is to be about and let every element in the lyrics and music present that idea and underscore it. To be consistent remember the rules for a good speech: tell the people what you are about to tell them, then tell them, and when you are concluding the song, tell them what you just told them. If you have something different to add, write another song! Be consistent; stick to one theme.

Flowing With the Music

Our last look at lyrics (I love alliteration) has to do with how the words flow with the music; in particular the melody. This is, to me, an instinctive thing and to overanalyze how this happens could be counter-productive. There are, however, some general principles that can help guide you in this process. Some of these are so obvious that they probably don't need much comment. I'm referring to things like making sure that the mood of the music matches the sentiment of the lyrics. If, for example, I was writing a brooding song about going through a difficult time, I probably wouldn't have a lot of major thirds in the melody with a reggae sounding major chord "happy" groove. There are glorious, ironic and clever exceptions to this but I think that's enough said about this particular piece of the songwriting puzzle.

There's an old saying, "You are what you eat." Putting that biblically: "You become like what (or Who) you behold." The same is true for your creative output. I am, musically speaking, a product of all the different songs, artists, styles and genres that I have listened to since I was born. For me that is a very wide spectrum: from Bach to the Beatles; Stevie Wonder to Lawrence Welk, Deep Purple to Simon and Garfunkel and all kinds of music in between. I am thankful that I have listened to a lot of different kinds of music and that I can find something to love about most genres. I am also grateful that God is the Redeemer. Even music that I have listened to that is, shall we say, less than wholesome, has come under the redemptive power of the blood of Jesus, and now His life, His songs, His melodies flow out of me.

Am I saying that because I am in Christ I will never write a bad song? Of course not. Have you heard the story about a man who said, "I want to play you a song that God gave me!" Then he played it. It was terrible, to put it mildly. So the poor dear at the receiving end of the song told someone, "I know why God gave him that song. God didn't want it!

Not every song we write will be a winner. Some are throwaways. The exercise of writing even the bad songs can be good practice for us. After all, the Bible says that, *"We have this treasure in earthen vessels that the excellency of the power may be of God and not of us."*

I once thought that to be the most effective in the Kingdom of God, I must disappear; that is, be devoid of personality. The beauty of the gospel, the good news that I have discovered is this: Jesus, through His obedient life as God become man, His death on a cross and His resurrection, gives me the grace and the power to be who I was originally created to be by my Father God when I receive Him by grace through faith. He sets me free, *in Him,* to be the real me. And the real me (and Jesus in me) shines through my life and the songs that I write. So live in the Lord and let His melody, music and Word flow through you. He is the Master Songwriter, the Singer and the Song!

A Closer Look At The Music

In this section we will look at four different attributes of the music itself:

1. *Memorable and singable melodies*
2. *Matching the mood of the lyric*
3. *Being creative and fresh*
4. *Using dynamics*

Memorable Melodies

Great melodies are those that are memorable, singable and have something intangible about them that grabs the listener. I personally believe that there are rivers of melodies flowing from heaven. My good friend Morris Chapman says, "We say we are songwriters, but we are really just song-*catchers*."

Some of the best songs that I have written have come with virtually no effort on my part. I just heard them in my head and in my heart, and in my spirit; and then, like taking heavenly dictation, I just began to sing or play them! I have also been playing the piano for over five decades and dedicated my life to being a musician and songwriter. So I don't want to trivialize or discount the importance of learning your instrument and being filled with the Spirit and the Word of God. It takes practice to make it seem effortless!

Now that we have acknowledged the Source of the melody, let's look at some characteristics of good melodies.

They are *singable*. Especially in the genre of praise and worship music, the song's melody should be fairly easy for a congregation to pick up. That means, also, that there should not be too wide a range. A good way to measure that is to not have more than an octave and a major second between the lowest note and the highest. Another word about range. The average female singer in most congregations gets uncomfortable singing above an octave above middle "C" for very long. The melody can touch on a "D" or even an "Eb" but much higher than that- especially if there are a lot of notes up there or they are held for a long time- most of the ladies will either stop singing or look for a more comfortable harmony part! A presentational song, as contrasted to a participatory one, can have more flexible parameters, but the above is a good general rule for the melodic range of a song. Sometimes I will be inspired to write in a certain key but then realize after finishing the song, that the original key is too high or occasionally too low. So I search to find the best congregational friendly key, and then change the chord sheet to reflect that new key.

Repetition is good, just don't overuse it. The song "Fill This Place" has a three note rhythmic and melodic theme that is fairly repetitious, and I think is a good example of a singable song.

Remember to allow rests in the melody. People have to breathe! Sometimes a song does well that has a very simplistic melody with some moving chord progressions underneath. For you keyboard players, try this:

Play a "**C**" major chord with your right hand. Start out with a "**C**" in the left hand as the bass note. Then, with the right hand continuing to play the "**C**" chord, play one bar at a time while playing different bass notes with the left. Notice how each change of the bass note brings a different mood or atmosphere. Well, the same thing can happen if you have a 2 or 3 note melody with differing chord changes.

Again, *Fill This Place*-The first two lines: *"Fill this place…with the praise"* are sung with exactly the same melody notes, only the chords underneath are changing. This does at least two things; it provides an easy-to-learn, memorable melody, and there is a dynamic and creative tension that is underscored by the movement of the chord changes. A complicated melody has its place in some songs, but for the purpose of encouraging the average congregational member to sing along, make your melody memorable, easy-to-learn, with a comfortable range and singable.

More About Chords

It is beyond the scope of this book to go into intricate detail about chord progressions, jazz chords, inversions, voicings and all the different components of chords, but let's cover some basics.

Music is like a living thing. It grows and changes, it has evolved over the centuries and is still doing so. I think that is because God is passionate about communication, because He values His relationship with us and our relationship with each other. What's that got to do with chord progressions? I am glad you asked!

In the kingdom of God, there are at least five purposes for music.

Music:

1. Is used by the Holy Spirit to communicate with us

2. Helps us communicate with each other

3. Enables us to express ourselves and to connect with our emotions and connect with our inner man (our spirit)

4. Breaks down emotional defenses and prepares our hearts to receive the Word of God. Let me add that this means not only the preached word but the Word of God that may reside in the song itself-even in instrumental music. Because music can convey the very Life of Jesus, who is the Living Word of God, all kinds of wonderful and powerful things can happen when a musician plays under the inspiration and anointing of the Holy Spirit. People are set free from bondages; they are healed; they are delivered from demonic oppression, and more!

5. Has within it a gift of memory. God put that gift of memory in music to help His people remember His Word, His works and His faithfulness.

With the above purposes of music in mind, let's look at how chords have evolved over the years.

The easiest example is the Five chord. In earlier generations, if a song had a simple progression like One/ Four/ Five, the Five chord was generally a dominant 7 chord. In the key of **C** the Five chord would be a **G7** and would contain the notes **G, B, D** and **F,** which is the dominant 7 note. Borrowing from classical music's influence, the **G7** chord, especially the **"F"** note, would strongly cause the listener to want to hear it resolve to a **C** major chord. Today, though it is still in use, most contemporary praise and worship songs would use a Four chord with a Five in the bass (in this key an **"F"** over **"G"** or **F/G**) or, even more often, a **G** without a 3rd or **G+2** (**Gsus2**) chord. It's not that the other chord, the **G7**, is musically wrong, it just, in most cases, sounds dated.

A lot of music nowadays uses the **+2** chord as a substitute for the major chord with a major 3rd in it. Why is that? I have my theories; for now let's just say that sounds evolve. They both reflect and forecast the future of the culture.

Another aspect of chord changes involves the use of the bass note. In the good old days (not that long ago) the bass note was, most of the time, the root of the chord. In other words if the chord was an "E" chord, then the bass note was an "E." Because of the evolution of music (don't let that word scare you; God created music and the word evolution simply means changing) the role of the bass note has changed too. There are really cool bass sounds that one can emphasize with synthesizers (say that three times real fast) that really add a lot to the sound of the music and chords in particular. A lot of modern music, for example, features the 3rd or the 6th note of the chord in the bass. In the verse of my song **"A New Anointing For A New Day"** the first two chords of the verse don't have the root of the chords in the bass. Instead of (in the key of **"E"**)

B   **A**   **E**

The oil from yesterday has gone stale...

I have put a different bass note, it sounds more contemporary:

B/D# bass   **A/C#** bass   **E+2**

The oil from yesterday has gone stale...

and notice that we made the "E" chord a "plus 2" (or **Esus2**) for even more of a "today" sound.

Of course, these kinds of musical treatments are subjective, the best thing for you to remember in writing songs is to use what sounds and chords sound and feel the best to you. As you grow in your musical proficiency and preferences, the important thing to remember is that music sounds best when it comes from your heart-when it is an authentic expression of who God made you to be!

Here is one more thing about chord changes and musical composition. Using great synthesizer sounds and digital effects for guitars and keyboards, and drum loops can aid you in the creative process. I can sit at a keyboard and play one patch (particular keyboard sound) and it will evoke in me a mood or suggest a melody or chord pattern, even lyrics! Then I can change the sound, and the mood changes. The main thing to remember, however, is that these effects, sounds and loops, etc., are aids to help the songwriter to tap into the flow. The most important elements in a good song are still the words and music. *The tools are not the flow; the flow is the flow!*

Something can sound cool and do absolutely nothing for somebody who needs encouragement from God. There is no substitute for the anointing of the Holy Spirit! One friend of mine reverently calls the anointing *"The Thing."* To paraphrase an old saying about jazz; "It don't mean a thing if it ain't got...*The Thing!*"

I've Got Rhythm

There was song that was a popular song on the radio in the U.S. a few decades ago by Christopher Cross called "Sailing."

Michael Omartian was the keyboard player, arranger and producer of that hit single. The song, in my opinion, was a watershed event for much of pop music because of the rhythmic, flowing chord changes. Some of you remember it.

"Sailing... take me away..."

When writing songs, tempo and rhythm must be conducive to the flow of the lyrics, and to the emotional feel of the song. Too slow and the song loses momentum and fails to capture the listener. Too fast and moments of creative genius are lost in the hurry. Just like Goldilocks and her porridge, there is a groove that is just right for the song. Find the right tempo; use the right chord inversions; find the common tones that stay the same in most or all of the chords to your song. Learn to play patterns, like the mesmerizing pattern of the chord changes played by the keyboard and guitar on "Sailing." (You younger writers that perhaps haven't heard that song may want to download it or youtube it to hear what I am talking about).

Try changing the tempo of your new song. Slow it down or speed it up. The tempo may be just fine where it was when you got the original song idea or, by experimenting, you may find a tempo that works better. You may find that the first part of the song works better slow, even *rubato* (with a flowing slow tempo) then speeding up the song as the chorus comes. Be creative; play with it.

A word to inexperienced musicians-don't overplay. Less is definitely more when it comes to presenting your song or playing with a rhythm section. Sometimes giving chords the whole note value in a bar (that is, just playing the chord on beat one and holding it for four beats) can be a great way to establish dramatic tension. Then, as the song builds, you can start playing quarter note chords to give the song a walking feel or the feeling of movement. Again, overplaying the instrument actually detracts from the song. Less is more.

As I write this I am reminded of an episode of the American television program "Frasier" in which the main character, Frasier, has decided to write a jingle to introduce his radio show. When he first talked about the idea with his brother Niles, (these guys are hilarious as they play Seattle sophisticates: Dr. Frasier and Dr. Niles Crane) Frasier had decided that a simple, short song accompanied by only one or two instruments would be the best.

He smugly told Niles, "After all, less is more."

In typical Frasier fashion, however, the more he got into writing and producing the song, the more instruments and singers began filling up the studio that he booked for the recording session. When Niles walked into the session and saw a whole orchestra and choir for what was supposed to have been a simple jingle, he asked his brother, "What happened to less is more?"

Impishly, Frasier turned to Niles and said, "Oh Niles, if less is more, think of how much more *more* will be!" I love it.

By the way, the sit-com ends with the radio station manager choosing to use Frasier's father Martin's simple jingle instead of Frasier's over-the-top production. Sometimes a simple guitar-vocal or keyboard-vocal demo is the best way to present your song.

Even when you utilize the amazing digital recording capabilities available today, resist the temptation to "Frasier-ize" your song. Don't overdo it!

Holy Desperation, A New Anointing, Egypt

Stories Behind the Songs

I have traveled extensively for the past 30 years as a full-time music minister, with the exception of three years on staff as worship pastor of a local church. Many times I have learned things about God or myself or life in these adventures. Sometimes I have to pinch myself to see if this Mississippi boy is really in Abuja, Nigeria or St. Petersburg, Russia or Indonesia, Kuwait, Greece, Italy, Singapore, Ukraine, Latvia- the list goes on.

I have been inspired to write songs in almost every nation I have been in, and I appreciate the Holy Spirit for helping me to hear and capture (catch) those songs. A lot of times the Lord will teach me valuable lessons from the songs He gives to me and through me. I want to write about two such songs that you will see are somehow connected.

I was in the United States, in San Antonio, Texas for a conference at a church that has come to be known as "The Oasis." One of the things about mid-week conferences is that the daytime sessions are difficult for people who have jobs to come to, therefore those sessions are usually less crowded than later on in the week. They are also, for whatever reason, some of the best sessions in the conference.

Here is the setting; we were in a morning session Wednesday of the conference. We had worshipped the Lord through song and it was time for the speaker. This morning featured a special guest speaker from the U.K. His name was Warrick Shenton. There was a special sense of expectation as he came to the podium. He began his message by saying that the Lord had led him to resign his position as the General Superintendent of a denomination in the U.K. This man, in his mid-sixties, began to tell us humbly that he didn't have many preaching meetings on his schedule, (all of us full-time ministers realized that he meant no obvious source of income) and that he didn't know what the future held for him. He tearfully continued, "But all of that doesn't matter because I have a *holy desperation* to know him!"

Rev. Shenton then began to deliver a powerful word- that it is the goodness of God when He allows us to become hungry and thirsty, indeed desperate for Him; and that despite all the potential distractions and attempts that we make to find our joy elsewhere, even in ministry, Jesus alone fully satisfies the longing of our hearts. It was powerful preaching, and as I was listening to him, I was also listening to Someone Else.

As he spoke the words *holy desperation*, the heavenly dictation light came on in my spirit. I got my pen and paper and began to write down what I was hearing. I heard everything about the song in the spirit realm (which is much louder than the audible realm). I heard the words, the chords, the string arrangement (especially the plaintive cellos and double basses) everything.

Because of the Spirit-led nature of this particular conference, and because those of us who were ministering that week had been given a green light by the leadership to share if the Holy Spirit gave us something to share, I went to the piano at the end of the message and began to sing what I felt that the Lord had just given me:

Holy Desperation

Holy desperation deep within my soul
A longing and a yearning
The sacred desolation of my own control
A holy fire is burning
Blessed are the barren for they will give birth
To the purpose of the Father as heaven comes to earth
Oh rend the skies and tear my heart!
Remove the veil from the face of Your bride and

Kiss me with the kisses of your mouth Oh Lord
Let me know the joy of holy abandon
O kiss me speak to me Lover of my soul
Oh the new wine
Oh the body and the blood
Blessed holy desperation
The Bride and Groom in the consummation

I realize that this all may sound dramatic. It was! But that is just half of the story. Now let's flash forward one year. We are again in San Antonio, at the same church, the same conference, the same sparsely attended Wednesday session, and even the same speaker as the previous year. After the praise and worship, Warrick Shenton again approached the pulpit. He began, "Last year I preached a message about having a holy desperation and when I was through speaking this brother here (he pointed at me) got up to the piano and *sang* the message! I have told people everywhere I have traveled about it, and it is one of the most remarkable things that I seen in forty years of ministry... but Dave here (now he approaches me and gently puts his finger on my chest) could go a whole year on the anointing that is in that song, and he could sell his tapes and CDs... but David here needs a new anointing for a new day!"

He then went on to tell the people that he was just using me and the song as an example. Actually, he was pretty accurate! Over that past year as I traveled and ministered, if I came to a place in the service where there was a lull, or it seemed that things weren't going so well, I would begin to sing "Holy Desperation" and... wow, immediately the atmosphere seemed to change and people began to respond.

As I began to offer a quiet and very real prayer of repentance, Rev. Shenton started preaching his message for the conference. He described how the cross that Jesus died on hung in the marketplace, in an open area in Jerusalem that people walking by could see. He then shared how the church has adopted certain paradigms of presenting the gospel to people that worked in days gone by. But God was beginning to pour out a new anointing for a new day, to get the truth about God into the marketplace and that if the Body of Christ, the church, didn't wake up to the fact that this is a new day, they would even begin to oppose the move of the Holy Spirit and criticize people who were being creative in their presentations of the gospel!

Well, it happened again. While he was speaking, (and after I told the Lord that I was sorry for leaning on yesterday's anointing and on my previous ministry experience) I started taking dictation from the Holy Spirit again. I finished the song during the message and, just like I did the previous year, got up and sang the new song:

A New Anointing For a New Day

The oil from yesterday has gone stale
And the strength that I once trusted in has failed
But Your fresh Word has been spoken
And my proud heart has been broken
So once again I come behind the veil, asking for

A new anointing for a new day
Oh Lord let it pour
A new anointing for a new day
To carry the glory of the Lord
Carry the glory of the Lord

Oh Holy Fragrance, Sweet Perfume
All Consuming Fire fill this room
No more living in yesterday's grace
O Lord pour Your power and Your
Passion for Your purposes today!

I could relate many more stories about how I have been inspired to write some of the songs I have written through the miles and the years, but let me share just one more with you.

Took Me Out Of Egypt

It was April of 1987. I was doing a concert at a friend's church in Reno, Nevada in the United States. The evening concert went well, and after it was over some of us went to my pastor friend's home for some fellowship and food. A young man walked up to me and told me how much he enjoyed the concert. Then he said this, "I particularly appreciated you singing the song 'Took Me Out Of Egypt.' He continued, "As a matter of fact, I heard that song on the radio in January."

At this, my eyebrows raised slightly.

"Are you sure you heard the song in January?" I asked. I had a good reason for asking that question.

"Yes, it was January. I am sure of it, and I remember it because I was at a low point in my life and I needed to hear something encouraging from the Lord. So I turned on the radio; even though there are no Christian radio stations that I can pick up on my radio in northern California where I live. As I turned the dial, all of a sudden I heard a DJ say, "Now here's a new song by David Baroni: Took Me Out of Egypt." As I heard that song, it was just what I needed to hear at the time. It's so nice to be able to hear the song again and I want to thank you.

I was still skeptical, with good reason. I went to get the day planner that I carried everywhere. I opened up to the day that I wrote the song. I showed it to the young man whose name was Rob.

"Rob, is this the song you heard on the radio in January of 1987?" I asked.

"Yes, that is the song."

"Rob, look above the lyrics to the date in my day planner. What is the date that I wrote the song?"

He stammered a bit… "F-F- February 17th, 1987!"

This young man (who is very sane and solid) heard a song that had not been *written* yet, much less recorded, on a radio station that doesn't exist. He heard the song *one month before it was written!* Boy, would I have liked to have heard that version! My pastor friend Mike spoke up.

"David, God already has all these songs written in heaven, and He decided that Rob needed to hear this song before He gave it to you!"

I know it sounds hard to believe. I was there and it still sounds strange, but God can do the impossible. He is not bound by time. There is one more intriguing element to this story.

Rob began to research Christian radio stations and found out that at one time there had been a Christian station at the point on the dial where he had heard the song. However, it had gone out of business *one year prior to playing the song "Took Me Out of Egypt!"* This reminds us that, as believers in

Christ led by the Spirit of God we are not limited to just the physical realm. By God's grace we can, in the words of Christian author George Warnock, "See the invisible, hear the inaudible, hold the intangible, declare the unspeakable, explore the unsearchable and do the impossible through Christ who lives in us!" I don't want to limit God through unbelief or by leaning to my own understanding. How about you? The Word says, *"The just shall live by faith, and faith is the substance of things hoped for, the evidence of things not seen."*

I am grateful that God is patient with us. He is helping us to have our minds renewed so that we can live in expectation of the unexpected in this great adventure of eternal intimacy with Christ!

Took Me Out of Egypt

Lord I feel so empty, seems like we're so far apart
Even though some may applaud me
You alone can see my heart
You don't look at my achievements or my ability
All you really want is all of me

And though it frightens me to give up my control
There is only room for one King in the throneroom
of my soul

Lord You took me out of Egypt
Now take Egypt out of me
You delivered me from Pharoah
Now set me free from me
Let my heart become a Promised Land
Where the desert used to be
Lord You took me out of Egypt
Now take Egypt out of me

Some Practical Tips

Thank you for coming with me on this journey into the world of songwriting. Now I want us to briefly examine some of the purposes for your songs. Let's ask this question: **Who is the song for?**

1. *The individual- You and God!*
2. *Congregation(s)*
3. *A Conference or special meetings*
4. *The mainstream marketplace*
5. *The nations*

The Prophetic Song

Presents a "Rhema" word - a right now fresh, relevant word from the Lord. It is usually inspired spontaneously, though it doesn't have to be spontaneously inspired to be prophetic. It can be vocal or instrumental. In a simple definition, to be prophetic is to see, hear and speak or sing from God's perspective and is only possible by the Holy Spirit.

Finally, I want to give you some helpful, practical suggestions as you work on your songs and grow musically.

<u>Practical tips for growing in Songwriting:</u>

1. **Listen** to the Spirit and Word of God, teaching/preaching, music.

2. **Co-write.** Find someone of like spirit, and write together, blending your strengths and weaknesses.

3. **Learn to discern** when a song is not just a good song but a "God-song."

4. **Be filled** with the Word and Spirit. Read the Psalms, carry a song in your heart always!

5. **Write it down or record it.** Not every idea for a song is a winner, but sometimes the Lord will inspire you when you least expect it!

6. **Hold your gifts loosely.** Let the Lord help you with your motives.

7. **Find your identity in who you are in Christ** and not in your musical/ songwriting (or any other) gifts.

Thank you so much for reading this book. As you practice its principles and listen to the Voice of your Creator, may the creative gifts that are inside of you flow like a river as you write the songs you were born to write!

THANK YOU!

I want to give a special thank you to the people who have listened to my songs over the years. Thanks for the emails, the smiles, the prayers and the encouragement. Thanks for buying the CDs and downloads and reminding me of how blessed I am to share this music. Feel free to email me at david@davidbaroni.com

Social Media:
Twitter   *@davidbaroni*
Facebook: *http://bit.ly/DBaroniartist*
Website: *davidbaroni.com*
Youtube: *https://www.youtube.com/jazzprchr*

You may also enjoy my other books:
Creative In The Image of God
Creative In The Image of God audiobook
Dreams Kings and Unseen Things
Dreams Kings and Unseen Things audiobook
The Jazz Preacher
From Rita Baroni: Fragrance of Grace

Made in the USA
Columbia, SC
23 February 2020